Written by Craig Robert Carey
Illustrated by Marc and
Isidre Mones

FIRE

Tonka

FIREBOAT 2

2

Exact Action

SCHOLASTIC INC.

New York Toronto London Auckland Sydney
Mexico City New Delhi Hong Kong Buenos Aires

HASBRO and its logo and TONKA are trademarks of Hasbro and are used with permission.
© 2006 Hasbro. All Rights Reserved.

Published by Scholastic Inc.
SCHOLASTIC and associated logos are trademarks and/or registered trademarks of Scholastic Inc.

ISBN 0-439-78964-8

12 11 10 9 8 7 6 5 4   9 10/0

Designed by Maria Stasavage

Printed in the U.S.A.
First printing, March 2006

These vehicles are built for an **EXACT** purpose — they do one job, and they do it really well.

The **street sweeper** keeps the roads clean. It has superpowerful brushes and a big vacuum to suck up the litter.

The **garbage truck** also keeps the streets clean. It carries away rubbish from trash cans and Dumpsters. Most garbage trucks smash the trash to make room for more.

The **road reclaimer** doesn't keep the street clean — it chews it up! It pulverizes the top layer of old roads into small pieces.

The reclaimer adds water to the new mix and lays it back down so a compactor can smooth it out. Then a crew resurfaces the road.

The **grader** is a very important vehicle for building a new road. It makes the ground surface perfectly smooth so roads can be built flat.

Graders also level the ground before construction of a new building begins. Some graders' blades are more than 20 feet wide!

Armored vans transport money between banks and businesses. They are protected by metal plates and bulletproof glass to prevent thieves from breaking in.

In an emergency, the fire department often calls in the **rescue truck**. It's a huge rolling toolbox, loaded with every tool a firefighter might need.

When disaster strikes an airport, the **Aircraft Rescue and Fire Fighting trucks** zoom into action. Some ARFF trucks have special nozzles sharp enough to pierce a metal fuselage.

ARFF trucks can drive almost anywhere — whether there's a road or not!

A **fireboat** is another vehicle firefighters use in special situations. It rescues people in the water, puts out fires on other boats, and sprays water onto buildings on shore.

FIRE

FIREBOAT 2

Tonka®

The fireboat won't run out of water — it pumps right from the river or lake. Some fireboats pump more than 20,000 gallons a minute!

The **thresher** is a special vehicle that cuts down wheat or oats in huge fields.

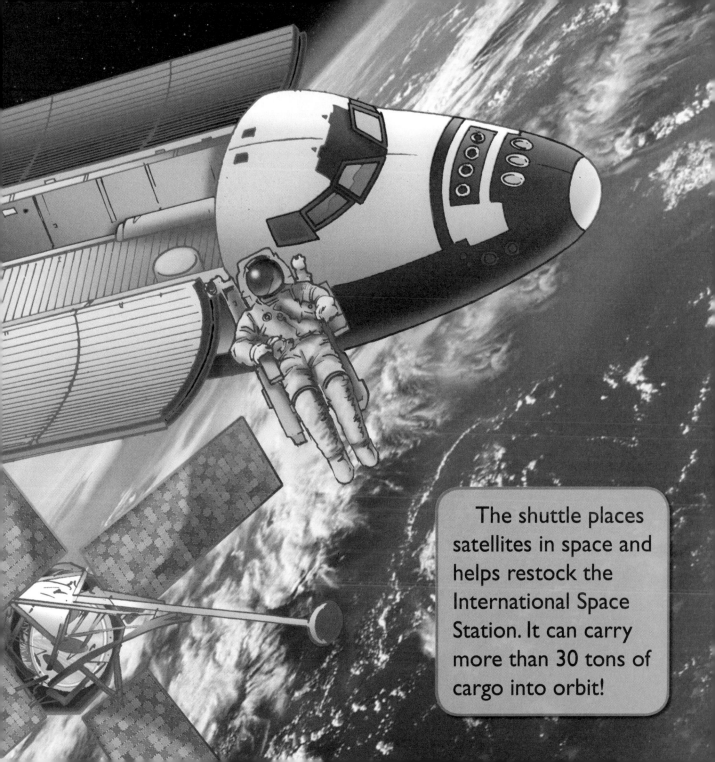

The shuttle places satellites in space and helps restock the International Space Station. It can carry more than 30 tons of cargo into orbit!